7
BIG
QUESTIONS

7 BIG QUESTIONS

Your Life Depends On

William J. Edgar

Crown & Covenant
PUBLICATIONS

© 2020 William J. Edgar,
Crown & Covenant Publications
7408 Penn Avenue
Pittsburgh, PA 15208
crownandcovenant.com

ISBN: 978-1-943017-33-1
e-book: 978-1-943017-34-8
Library of Congress Control Number: 2020935183

Printed in the United States of America

Unless otherwise noted, all Scripture quotations in this publication are from the Good News Translation in Today's English Version—Second Edition Copyright © 1992 by American Bible Society. Used by Permission.

The text is set in Chaparral Pro 12/14, and heads in Avenir Next Condensed.

I dedicate this book to the students, faculty, and administration of Geneva College in Beaver Falls, Pennsylvania. In 2015–16, they listened attentively (mostly) to oral versions of this book's chapters delivered from a few notes. Knowing them, their questions and their needs, helped me to frame each talk.

I dedicate this book to the people of the Broomall Reformed Presbyterian Church near Philadelphia where I preached the first four chapters in 2014.

I dedicate this book to my high school students and fellow teachers at East High School in West Chester, Pennsylvania, who unknowingly supplied me with countless stories over the years, a few of which are in this book.

And I thank my Lord for the varied life he has given me, with twists and turns I could not have anticipated, including writing this book. As I prepared and delivered these talks at Geneva, I intended each to stand by itself; they were not delivered in the order they appear in this book. But after I finished them, I realized the questions I addressed dealt with central Christian teachings: God the Creator, Satan the tempter, man the sinner, life and death, and Jesus our sacrifice for sin and living Savior.
To him be all glory and praise.

7 BIG QUESTIONS

Introduction ix

1. Satan: Did God Really Say? 1
2. God: Where Are You? 7
3. Isaac: Where Is the Lamb? 15
4. Jacob and Joseph: Am I in the Place of God? 23

   The Story of Israel from Joseph to Jesus's Birth 29

5. Astrologers: Where Is the Baby Born to Be
   King of the Jews? 35
6. Jesus: Do You Want to Be Healed? 41
7. Angel: Why Are You Looking among the Dead
   for One Who Is Alive? 47

Questions for Discussion 55

INTRODUCTION

THIS BOOK DOES not deal with questions people often ask, such as, "Is there a God?" It does not summarize the Bible's teaching, like the *Westminster Shorter Catechism* does, with questions like, "What is the chief end of man?" (Question 1) or "What is God?" (Question 4). Instead, it considers seven questions asked in the Bible. Loudly or softly, you hear each question throughout your life. Together, they describe the human condition and what God has done about it. Read this short book at a leisurely pace, and ask yourself, "How do I hear, and how do I answer, each question?"

I extend my thanks to early readers who made helpful suggestions: first my wife, Gretchen; then my daughter Betsy; next three of her school-aged children, Emma, Mary, and Isaac; and finally my son Alex and his wife, Susan.

1

SATAN

"DID GOD REALLY SAY"

TEACHERS IN THE high school I taught in for thirty years strictly enforced one school rule: never wear a hat in school—not in class, not in the hallway, not in the lunchroom, nowhere. When a student wanted to defy authority, he—and sometimes she—kept the hat on. Some of my sharpest confrontations with students concerned hats. Students complained the rule was irrational. Why forbid wearing hats? Actually, the rule's point was quite clear: it was the sign and symbol of the school's authority.

When the Creator made Man, male and female, he put them into a walled Garden fit for a king in the land of Eden and gave them one rule. They could eat from any tree in the Garden except the one in the middle, the Tree of the Knowledge of Good and Evil. If they disobeyed and ate its fruit, they would die (Genesis 2:7–9, 15–17). That forbidden Tree was the sign that God is God, and we are not, just like the hat rule showed students that they did not run the school.

A third personage entered the Garden. "The snake was the most cunning animal that the LORD God had made. It asked the woman, 'Did God really tell you not to eat fruit from any tree in the Garden?'" (Genesis 3:1) The snake's oily pretend-friend question slyly insinuated that God was unreasonable and the enemy of happiness. "We may eat the fruit of any tree in the garden," the woman answered, "except the tree in the middle of it. God told us not to eat the fruit of that tree or even touch it; if we do, we will die" (Genesis 3:2–3). The "or touch" was her addition to God's command, hinting that she might be ready to consider God unfair.

Then the snake struck. "That's not true; you will not die. God said that because he knows that when you eat it, you will be like God and know what is good and what is bad" (Genesis 3:4–5). Choosing to believe her new "friend" that God was selfish for wanting to deny them wisdom and a liar who would not really carry out his threat of death, the woman ate the forbidden tree's fruit and gave some to Adam who was with her. He ate it too.

All around us, we hear that first question asked in the Bible: "Did God really say?" We hear the question from friends, enemies, books, and the internet. Most dangerously, we hear it in our own thoughts. Like the snake, the questioner always suggests that God is unreasonable. Did God really say, "You shall love your enemies?" Really? *My enemies?* Did God really say, "In everything give thanks?" Really? *I just lost my job!* Did God really say, "Pray for all in authority?" Really? *This president?* Did God really say, "No sex outside of marriage?" Really? *But we are mutually consenting adults.* When do these questions most easily entice us? When a real enemy has hurt us, when life has turned sour, when our emotions and hormones are aroused, or when something looks really, really attractive, then we want to say, "No, God cannot have commanded that, and it won't hurt me!"

When we hear, "Did God really say?" and also a reassuring, "You won't get hurt," we willfully deceive ourselves. Built into everyone's conscience is this truth: "Everyone must die once, and after that be judged by God" (Hebrews 9:27). That is why when atheists do what they know is wrong, they may silently say, "Well, God—if you are there—you'll forgive me," as a formerly atheist friend of mine said he used to do. Still, we long for the power and fame that go with Satan's promise, "You will be like God," and all too often go ahead and disobey God. All sons of Adam and daughters of Eve are born infected with the snake's rebellious spirit and are receptive to the question, "Did God really say?"

Who is the snake that brought trouble into God's good world? The Bible has many names for it. It is Satan, meaning "enemy," who trips us (Matthew 16:23; Acts 5:3). It is the dragon (Revelation 12:9). It is the Evil One from whom Christians pray to be delivered (Matthew 6:13). It is the god of this world and the prince of the power of the air (2 Corinthians 4:4; Ephesians 2:2). It is the devil, an accuser and slanderer (Revelation 12:10; Job 1:6). The snake is a liar and the father of lies who tempts people into sin, sorrow, and death. And it is a murderer (John 8:44).

Our enemy roars like a lion when it can, enslaving countries where God has been forgotten with fears of demons constantly needing to be appeased. I remember vividly a video of new Christians in a village in South Sudan exultantly dancing around a burning pile of their wooden, demonic gods of whom they were no longer afraid, because they now believed in one stronger than their old idols: Jesus.

Sometimes Satan appears as an angel of light, mostly within Christian churches (2 Corinthians 11:14). As within the garden, likewise in Christian families and churches, Satan dares not appear as a lion, so he leads people astray by asking, "Did God really say?" He suggests reasons for disregarding Jesus's command to love our enemies, pray for all in authority, honor our parents, or to hate adultery. Satan is the sleazy "friend," saying of God's threats, "It ain't necessarily so. In fact, it ain't so! So go ahead, obey your instincts, and feed your desires. Do what feels good and be true to yourself. Be authentic!"

The parents of one of my grandsons allow him a piece of bubble gum a day. He and his brothers can take their piece whenever they choose from a freely accessible bag. The four-year-old recently said to his mother, "Satan said to me, 'Take two. No one will know.'" His mother asked, "And what did you do?" "I ignored him," he answered, a good response to Satan's promise that two pieces of bubblegum would bring him extra happiness and that no one would ever know. Jesus was firmer! When Satan tempted him, he answered with God's Word and then told Satan, "Get out of here" (Matthew 4:10; 16:23).

Alert children and adults recognize Satan's voice when it whispers, "Don't worry, no one will ever know, there will be no punishment, and did God really say that anyway?" Wise is the one who ignores the snake's voice. Stronger is the one who tells Satan, "Get lost." "Resist the devil and he will run away from you" (James 4:7). Recognize the devil's voice, ignore it, and tell Satan to go away. But remember, he will be back. He left even Jesus only "for a while" (Luke 4:13).

The first woman followed the advice of her new friend, the snake. She ate the forbidden fruit, and so did her husband. Then their eyes were opened. They knew the difference between good and evil, but sadly from evil's side. Immediately, they hid from God.

Sinful people hide from God in many ways. They invent new gods for themselves and worship creatures made by the living God (Romans 1:18–23). They turn the true God into Santa Claus who gives presents whether they are naughty or nice. They say, "There is no God; God doesn't exist," and then get angry with him for not existing. They shove thoughts of God out of their minds when such thoughts intrude. They distract themselves with drugs, music, and electronic devices, so they are never left alone with their own thoughts. They pretend to know that the universe made itself and that the unfathomable complexity of life happened by chance. They make themselves their own god, give themselves their own rules, and hope that science can find a way to make them eternal. They try to live up to Satan's promise, that "you will be as God." But they can't, always ending up disillusioned, unhappy, and finally dead.

People hide from God, they hide from themselves, and they may even hide from other people. It is not good for anyone to be alone, but Satan seeks to isolate us (Genesis 2:18). In our day, smartphones, Snapchat, and Instagram (Facebook and Twitter for old folks) promise infinite connectivity to other people, but in fact they take away the human touch we people of flesh and blood need. Even worse, their constant distraction keeps us from hearing God.

Disobedient and alone, the first man and woman suddenly knew they were naked. They were not like God at all! To cover their vulnerability, they made pathetic clothing from fig leaves and hid from God. The snake, their chosen advisor and friend, did not help. He could not help. They were guilty, friendless, lost, and facing death.

2

GOD
"WHERE ARE YOU"?

GENESIS 3:8–24

HIGH SCHOOL STUDENTS sometimes fall asleep in class and need to be awakened. One teacher I knew would kneel in front of Sleeper, have the person behind them tap Sleeper on shoulder, so when their eyes opened, there were Teacher's eyes staring into theirs. Another teacher grabbed Sleeper's desk, shook hard, and screamed, "Earthquake!" My method was fake, sticky-sweet sympathy. "You're really tired aren't you? Go ahead, put your head down and sleep. I'll help you." Then I would sing, "Lullaby, and good night, with roses bedight...." Up came the face with a look saying, "Please stop. Now! Please! I'll stay awake. I promise." By April Fool's Day, however, teachers often let chronic sleepers sleep, meaning, "Have it your own way. We give up on you. Go ahead and fail."

After Eve and Adam had broken God's rule and eaten the forbidden fruit, they acted like sleeping students. They hid from God. How awful if God had let them have their own way and stay hidden. But he didn't. He called, "Where are you?" and out of hiding they came. Despite their disobedience, God was not finished with them. He asked the man, "Did you eat the fruit that I told you not to eat?" (Genesis 3:11) The man claimed victim status and shifted his blame onto both his wife and God: "The woman you put here with me, she gave me the fruit, and I ate it" (Genesis 3:12). The woman also blame-shifted. "The snake tricked me into eating it" (Genesis 3:13). However, their trying to evade responsibility by blaming someone else did not fool God.

First, God cursed the snake. He and the woman would be enemies, as would their offspring. The serpent's child would injure the woman's child, biting its heel, and the woman's child would crush the serpent's head (Genesis 3:15). That promise extends to all of the woman's children throughout history, as Paul wrote to the church in Rome: "And God, our source of peace, will soon crush Satan under your feet" (Romans 16:20).

Next, God spoke to the woman. She would long for her husband, but he would rule over her, and children would cause pain. Third, God spoke to the man, cursing the ground to produce thorns and weeds as well as food. The man would eat from it in sorrow all his life. Then, after hard lives, both the man and woman would die. From the soil they came, and to the soil they would return (Genesis 2:7; 3:19). Finally, God expelled the man and his wife from the garden in Eden and made it impossible to return.

Everyone hears the question, "Where are you?" We can't escape God because "in him we live and move and exist" (Acts 17:28). "How clearly the sky reveals God's glory," and his power and wisdom are seen in his creation (Psalm 19:1; Romans 1:19–20). The creation, in fact, practically screams at us, "Someone with immeasurable intelligence and power designed and made me." A single-celled creature is as complex as a Boeing 747 airplane, and unlike the airplane it can reproduce itself over and over again.

Here is the story my wife, Gretchen, tells about how God kept asking her, "Where are you?" At a summer waitressing job, the inn owner told her, "You're bitter." She denied it mentally: "I'm not bitter. I'm a good person, and good people are not bitter." But she could hear, "Something is wrong with you." She did not know it then, but the accusation that she was a bitter person was God saying, "Where are you?"

Next summer, she heard a similar accusation. A co-worker said to her, "You're angry. You need God." Gretchen knew she was angry: at her divorced parents, at her bullying brother, at her alcoholic mother. Her co-worker continued, "You need God." There it was again. "Gretchen, where are you?"

Later that summer, my brother John invited Gretchen to work in the kitchen at White Lake Covenanter Camp, our church's campgrounds in New York State. The adults all knew she was not a believer. Everyone was kind to her. One day a tough girl of fourteen from Boston, who slept in the same cabin, came to her in tears. "Is it true you're not a Christian?" she asked. Gretchen told her it was true. More tears, and Gretchen knew the girl was crying for her. Tears break hearts sledgehammers can't touch. "Gretchen, where are you?"

The camp speaker one evening was Sam Boyle, a missionary in China and later Japan. Sam spoke about the philosophy of existentialism and Christian faith, explaining why existentialism provides no lasting answer to the human condition while Christianity does. His talks were not the fundamentalist, anti-intellectual caricature Gretchen thought was Christianity. "Gretchen, where are you?"

After we returned to Swarthmore College, Gretchen and I studied together in the library. We had endless arguments about whether Christianity was true. I thought I was getting nowhere, but unknown to me, Gretchen would go back to her dorm and try out my arguments on her roommate, who faithfully gave Gretchen's answers back to her. Throughout the fall of 1967, those answers began to sound thinner and thinner. "Gretchen, where are you?"

Over Christmas break, Gretchen read the Gospel of Mark. In Mark's Gospel, Gretchen met Jesus: the real Jesus, the historical Jesus—the Lord Jesus. He was not like other teachers. This was not Kahlil Gibran or Erich Fromm, 1960s gurus for muddled college students. Jesus spoke—and acted—with authority! And the question, "Gretchen, where are you?" became a divine command: "Gretchen, follow me." She did not want to, but her excuses were failing.

Finally, Gretchen wrote up her own philosophy of life and gave it to me to read. We talked about it, and she returned to her dorm realizing that when she said, "I have my own beliefs," they were nothing more than incoherent good intentions founded on air.

A few days later, we sat together in my dorm's lounge: "Any further questions?"

"No."

"Any further objections?"

"No."

"Are you ready to bow to Jesus Christ?" She did not want to come to God and got cute and giggly to try to distract me. But in the end, she knew she had to deal with Jesus, who would be her judge. So we knelt together, and she prayed to God. She would follow Jesus. Then, as she puts it, she went into a corner and sulked. Gretchen would be a Christian, but she didn't have to like it.

Later, when Gretchen read the English writer C. S. Lewis's description of his own conversion in *Surprised By Joy*, she recognized herself:

> You must picture me alone in that room in Magdalen, night after night, feeling, whenever my mind lifted even for a second from my work, the steady, unrelenting approach of Him whom I so earnestly desired not to meet. That which I greatly feared had at last come upon me. In the Trinity Term of 1929 I gave in, and admitted that God was God, and knelt and prayed: perhaps, that night, the most dejected and reluctant convert in all England. I did not then see what is now the most shining and obvious thing; the Divine humility which will accept a convert even on such terms. The Prodigal Son at least walked home on his own feet. But who can duly adore that Love which will open the high gates to a prodigal who is brought in kicking, struggling, resentful, and darting his eyes in every direction for a chance of escape?

As Gretchen matured in her faith, she remembered earlier times when God had called, "Where are you?" Beauty especially had aroused in her a longing she could neither explain nor hold on to: reading 1 Corinthians 13, the chapter on love; the junior girls singing carols at Christmas time while holding candles as they walked down the halls of Westtown School, her Quaker boarding school; some songs at the First Day School she went to when very young. "Gretchen, where are you?" Through beauty that touched her when she was young, love that she saw at White Lake Covenanter Camp, and the truth revealed in the Bible, God called Gretchen, "Where are you?" until finally his question became an inescapable command.

The first human pair answered God's question, "Where are you?" It was not a fun interview, and God had hard words for them both. But suppose Adam and Eve had continued hiding? They would then not have heard how the coming victory would be won over their enemy, the snake. They would have remained lonely, naked, and lost without Jesus, the Sun of Righteousness, who brings healing in his wings (Malachi 4:2).

In December 1968, Gretchen was baptized "in the name of the Father, and of the Son, and of the Holy Spirit, one God over all, blessed forever." We married the following June. Gretchen's big fear was that if she became a Christian, God would make her be a missionary. He did! In 1970, we went to the island of Cyprus. In 1974, war sent us home when Turkish airplanes bombed, rocketed, and strafed our city of Famagusta. We fled with our son, one-and-a-half-years old, and our daughter still in the womb, but with very little else. Being a missionary was good for Gretchen. Jesus has done her no wrong.

You, my reader, have heard God ask, "Where are you?" Everyone has heard that question in one form or another. In ancient times, God called the boy Samuel, who did not know it was God speaking. But the old priest Eli knew. He told Samuel, "Go back to bed; and if he calls you again, say, 'Speak, LORD, your servant is listening'" (1 Samuel 3:9). My now departed friend Christian Adjemian, a tenured college professor in linguistics with a national reputation, was discontented. He went to a psychiatrist for help. The psychiatrist told him, "Your problem is not psychological. It is spiritual." The professor then remembered that a student had invited him to church. "Professor, where are you?" So the professor stopped hiding and went looking for God, beginning at the church to which he had been invited, and found God in Jesus Christ.

How would the offspring of the woman crush the serpent? "Have many children, so that your descendants will live all over the earth," God had commanded the first two humans (Genesis 1:28). If there is no baby, then there is no one to crush the snake's head, and there is no hope. No baby, no future. So, barred from the garden, the ground cursed, and with children to be a source of pain, Eve bore Cain and then Abel. Cain, grown to be a man, brought God some crops he grew, and God rejected his offering. Abel brought God his best sheep for sacrifice, and God accepted it. Jealous and angry, Cain killed Abel, and God banished Cain to wander the earth. He was the son of the snake. Adam and Eve's next son, Seth, was the ancestor of Abraham, in whom all nations of the earth have been blessed (Genesis 12:3).

Everyone hears two questions, a falsely friendly one, "Did God really say?" and an accusing one, "Where are you?" The first question brings eternal death to those whom it leads astray. The accusing question leads to the sure promise of the resurrection of the body and eternal life to those who stop hiding from God and come to him in his way.

3

ISAAC

"WHERE IS THE LAMB"

GENESIS 22

MOST CHILDREN PLAY with a Slinky toy at some time or other. It goes down steps by itself. You can pull it long, let go, and it will spring back. But too soon a coil kinks, and the Slinky won't work properly. Neither children nor parents can fix it, no matter how hard they try. Since the first man and woman listened to the snake, the world is like a kinked Slinky.

Nature that gives life is often inhospitable since God cursed the ground because of sin. What's more, wars and strife never stop: from Cain killing Abel, to the bombing of Hiroshima, to the present. Frustratingly, every plan to get back to the paradise of the garden fails. No utopian community has ever succeeded. Politicians say, "We can put a man on the moon, but we can't...." Then they claim to have a plan that can. But the War on Drugs has failed. So has the War on Poverty. Here is what is wrong with the world: "God's anger is revealed from heaven against all the sin and evil of the people whose evil ways prevent the truth from being known" (Romans 1:18).

> For creation was condemned to lose its purpose, not of its own will, but because God willed it to be so. Yet there was the hope that creation itself would one day be set free from its slavery to decay and would share the glorious freedom of the children of God. For we know that up to the present time all of creation groans with pain, like the pain of childbirth. (Romans 8:20–22)

How can humanity escape God's wrath? There is only one way. By sacrifice! The penalty for disobedience in the garden was death, and only a death can satisfy God's justice. After the great flood killed all but Noah's family, he sacrificed animals to God. Then,

> the odor of the sacrifice pleased the LORD, and he said to himself, "Never again will I put the earth under a curse because of what people do; I know that from the time they are young their thoughts are evil. Never again will I destroy all living beings, as I have done this time. As long as the world exists, there will be a time for planting and a time for harvest. There will always be cold and heat, summer and winter, day and night. (Genesis 8:21–22)

The descendants of Noah, as they spread over the face of the earth, worshiped the Most High God with animal sacrifice. As they forgot him and turned to worship created things, they continued the practice of animal sacrifice, in some places supplementing it with human sacrifice.

When Isaac asked his father Abraham, "Where is the lamb for the burnt offering?" he was asking where was the sacrifice that would make them right with God and fix the broken world. Everyone hears that question: Where is the lamb to make things right and fix the world?

In our day, we don't phrase the question in terms of sacrifice, but we do ask, What will it take to fix the world? The tragedy of the twentieth century was that the blood of millions was shed to accomplish the goal of utopian communist or utopian nationalist dreams, which failed miserably. Communism is the god that failed, yet its utopian dream still attracts people, and the temptation to worship a nation's blood and soil is not dead.

God's command to Abraham to sacrifice his son Isaac as a burnt offering is one of the most shattering stories in the Bible. To understand it, we must imagine the world of 4,000 years ago. Abraham was born in the city of Ur on the Euphrates River, part of Iraq today. God told him to go to a new land, so he traveled north along the river until he came to Haran, in present-day southern Turkey. After his father Terah died, Abraham traveled to Canaan, where people sacrificed babies to their gods. Abraham went right through Canaan to Egypt, had an unfortunate adventure with Egypt's pharaoh involving Abraham's wife Sarah, and returned to Canaan a rich man. God was looking out for Abraham because God had chosen to make from him a great nation, with children as many as the stars in the sky (Genesis 12:1–3; 15:5). But at eighty-six, Abraham was childless, so Sarah gave him Hagar, her slave. Hagar bore a son, Ishmael. Abraham had his heir, and all seemed settled.

When Abraham was nearly a hundred, God told him he would have a son by his ninety-year-old wife Sarah, who laughed at the very thought of being a mother at her age. That son would inherit God's promises to Abraham. Despite her and Abraham's lack of faith, in due time Sarah bore a son and named him Isaac. Abraham sent Hagar and Ishmael away. Again, Abraham and his family lived peaceably at Beersheba on the edge of the desert. All seemed settled.

Then God came to Abraham to test him. "Take your son," God said, "your only son, Isaac, whom you love so much, and go to the land of Moriah. There on a mountain that I will show you, offer him as a sacrifice to me" (Genesis 22:2). Listen how Moses, the author of Genesis, makes us feel the horror of God's appalling demand: "Take your son, your only son, Isaac, whom you love so much..." Abraham obeyed promptly, taking servants, donkeys, firewood, and Isaac, on a three days' journey north through sparsely populated land to the place God would show him.

Use your imagination. Put yourself in Abraham's place on this journey of agony and death. Isaac, maybe ten years old, was on an adventure, running ahead and back, talking excitedly with his father and the servants. Abraham rode on a donkey. Night came, and they made camp. Isaac went to sleep, the servants took turns watching for lions, and Abraham looked at the Milky Way, bright with thousands of stars visible in a dark and unpolluted sky. Abraham surely pondered, "God promised to make my descendants as numerous as these stars. How? God wants my son Isaac as a sacrifice to him! Are the Canaanites correct after all to offer their children as sacrifices?" Canaanites were not the only ones in the ancient world to conclude that the gods wanted human sacrifice, since a human is far more valuable than a lamb or a goat. The Druids, Carthaginians, Aztecs,

Incas, and many more around the globe came to the same conclusion as the Canaanites and acted on it. Finally, Abraham fell asleep, full of love for Isaac his son, and dreading the morning.

The next day they traveled on. Isaac still ran and laughed on his adventure. The second night came, and again Abraham gazed at the stars. "God, who gave me a son in my old age, can bring him back to life," he thought (Hebrews 11:19). Abraham slept.

On the third day, they arrived at the mountain where Solomon's temple would later be built. Leaving the servants behind, Abraham and Isaac, his son whom he loved, climbed the hill.

> Abraham made Isaac carry the wood for the sacrifice, and he himself carried a knife and live coals for starting the fire. As they walked along together, Isaac said, "Father!" He answered, "Yes, my son?" Isaac asked, "I see that you have the coals and the wood, but where is the lamb for the sacrifice?" Abraham answered, "God himself will provide one." And the two of them walked on together. When they came to the place, which God had told him about, Abraham built an altar and arranged the wood on it, he tied up his son and placed him on the altar, on top of the wood. Then he picked up the knife to kill him. (Genesis 22:6–10)

Isaac's blood would run out, and Abraham would burn his son to God, as the Canaanites did with their children.

> But the angel of the LORD called to him from heaven, "Abraham, Abraham!" He answered, "Yes, here I am."
> "Don't hurt the boy or do anything to him," he said.

"Now I know that you honor and obey God, because
you have not kept back your only son from him." Abraham looked round and saw a ram caught in a bush by
its horns. He went and got it and offered it as a burnt
offering instead of his son. (Genesis 22:11–13)

From then on, Abraham's descendants knew that the
Canaanite way was not God's way. The Hebrews would con-
tinue with animal sacrifice. Hundreds of years later, when
the nation of Judah, which came from Abraham, began
imitating the Canaanites and sacrificed their own children,
God expelled them from Canaan into captivity in Babylon
(Deuteronomy 12:31; 18:9–12; Psalm 106:38; Jeremiah
19:4–5). They had forgotten what Abraham had said to
Isaac: "The LORD will provide."

More than a thousand years after Abraham, God promised through the prophet Isaiah that he would one day give
his chosen servant to Israel (Isaiah 42:1–9; 49:1–13). God's
servant would make things right between God and his people by dying for them. Here is how Isaiah described God's
servant:

It was the will of the LORD that his servant should
grow like a plant taking root in dry ground. He had no
dignity or beauty to make us take notice of him. There
was nothing attractive about him, nothing that would
draw us to him. We despised him and rejected him; he
endured suffering and pain. No one would even look
at him—we ignored him as if he were nothing. But
he endured the suffering that should have been ours,
the pain that we should have borne. All the while we
thought that his suffering was punishment sent by
God. But because of our sins he was wounded, beaten

because of the evil we did. We are healed by the punishment he suffered, made whole by the blows he received. All of us were like sheep that were lost, each of us going his own way. But the LORD made the punishment fall on him, the punishment all of us deserved. He was treated harshly, but endured it humbly; he never said a word. Like a lamb about to be slaughtered, like a sheep about to be sheared, he never said a word. He was arrested and sentenced and led off to die, and no one cared about his fate. He was put to death for the sins of our people. He was placed in a grave with the wicked, he was buried with the rich, even though he had never committed a crime or ever told a lie. (Isaiah 53:2–9)

God's final answer to Isaac's question "Father, where is the lamb?" came when God sent his Son, born of a woman, and told his legal father Joseph as well as his mother, Mary, to name him Jesus because he would save his people from their sins (Matthew 1:21; Luke 1:31). John the Baptist pointed out Jesus to his disciples, saying, "There is the Lamb of God, who takes away the sin of the world!" (John 1:29).

A friend of mine was a professional marriage counselor. Unhappy couples would ask her to help sort things out, and usually there was a significant amount of sin in their troubles. When wrongdoing came out, they would want to talk about how to deal with their guilty *feelings*. She would ask insistently, "Yes, but what are you going to do about your *guilt*?" Eventually, she would get the question she was waiting for: "Oh, all right. What do you do about *your* guilt?" Then she would tell them about Jesus.

All our lives we wonder, "Why is the world like a broken Slinky toy? Who will fix it?" Less loudly perhaps, we ask, "How can I be reconciled to God?" Only our Creator and

Judge can make us right with himself. His chosen means is the sacrifice of his own Son, a sacrifice Jesus freely made. "For God loved the world so much that he gave his only Son, so that everyone who believes in him may not die but have eternal life" (John 3:16).

The other answer to the question, "How can things be made right?" is to try to make the snake's lie, "You will be like God," come true. It is the path of corporate utopianism, where unimaginably rich and clever people decide how everyone else should live. It is the path of totalitarian utopianism in which political rulers play at being God. Such powerful people often want others to treat them as divine. Weaker people may flatter or plead with strong people to take God's place and save them. However, godly people refuse to be treated as divine. Only the Creator is God, and only he can fix what we have broken.

4

JACOB AND JOSEPH

"AM I IN THE PLACE OF GOD"

GENESIS 30:1-2; 50:15-21

INSCRIBED ON MY wedding ring is our family motto: "Except the LORD build the house, they labor in vain that build it" (Psalm 127:1 KJV). The motto reminds my wife and me of two things. First, hard work cannot guarantee success. Work we must, but without God's blessing, it will fail. There is no point, therefore, in living to work. Anyone pursuing a 24/7 career is a fool. Take a nap. The psalm continues: "It is useless to work so hard for a living, getting up early and going to bed late. For the LORD provides for those he loves, while they are asleep" (Psalm 127:2). Second, and even more importantly, the psalm reminds us that only God is God. We cannot plan for the future with consistent success, just like we cannot decide for ourselves what is right or wrong. The snake in the garden lied. We can never be "as God" (Genesis 3:5).

God's servants, therefore, have always refused to be treated as divine. When the Roman centurion Cornelius fell at Peter's feet to worship him, Peter immediately stopped him: "Stand up; I myself am only a man" (Acts 10:26). When a crowd in Lystra tried to sacrifice to Paul and Barnabas as gods, they ran into the crowd, shouting, "Why are you doing this? We ourselves are only human beings like you!" (Acts 14:15). Angels did the same. When the Apostle John fell at the feet of the angel speaking to him, the angel rebuked John. "Don't do it! I am a servant together with you and with your fellow believers, all those who hold to the truth that Jesus revealed. Worship God!" (Revelation 19:10).

On the other hand, when a crowd flattered King Herod's speech, "It isn't a man speaking, but a god," the true God punished Herod for accepting the praise. "At once the angel of the Lord struck Herod down, because he did not give honor to God" (Acts 12:22–23). When someone attributes to us god-like power, knowledge, authority, or respect, Christians should quickly say something like, "Stop! Don't treat me like I am God!"

Both Jacob and his son Joseph said exactly that, each in a quite different situation. Jacob's life as a young man was a mess. He had tricked his father, Isaac, into giving him the blessing belonging to his older twin, Esau, and then, when Esau threatened to kill him, he escaped to his Uncle Laban in far away Haran. At a well, he met Laban's gorgeous daughter Rachel and immediately fell in love with her. Laban made Jacob work seven years for her and then tricked the trickster by giving Jacob Rachel's homely older sister, Leah, as his wife. A few weeks later, Laban finally gave Rachel to Jacob as his wife, demanding yet seven more years of work.

Now Jacob had two wives: Rachel, whom he loved, and Leah, who gave him children. "Rachel had not borne Jacob any children, and so she became jealous of Leah and said to Jacob, 'Give me children, or I will die'" (Genesis 30:1). Jacob replied angrily, but correctly, "Am I in the place of God, who has kept you from having children?" (Genesis 30:2 NIV).

Jacob might have answered otherwise, "I'm sorry, Rachel dear. I know how much you want a son. We'll keep trying." He might have said to his favored-but-childless wife what another man named Elkanah awkwardly said in the same situation to his favored wife, "Hannah, why are you crying? Why won't you eat? Why are you always so sad? Don't I mean more to you than ten sons?" (1 Samuel 1:8). But Jacob's answer was exactly on the mark. Rachel was demanding what only God could accomplish—give her a child—and doing it in drama-queen style too: "or I will die." Believers should not allow even their wives, or husbands, to put them in the place of God.

Decades later, Jacob's favorite son Joseph also refused to be put in the place of God, but in very different circumstances than Jacob's. His jealous half-brothers had cruelly sold Joseph into slavery in Egypt, but after many trials God made him a ruler there instead of a slave. When seven years of famine came following seven years of abundant crops, Joseph brought his entire extended family, seventy in all, to live in Egypt.

After their father Jacob died, Joseph's half-brothers feared that he would finally take revenge for their evil treatment of him, so they made up a story that their father's last words were a plea to Joseph not to punish his brothers. They fell at Joseph's feet. "But Joseph said to them, 'Don't be afraid. Am I in the place of God? You intended to harm me, but God intended it for good to accomplish what is now being done, the saving of many lives'"(Genesis 50:19–20 NIV). To punish his brothers would have been pure vengeance, and vengeance belongs only to God.

God tells us directly not to take our own revenge:

> If someone has done you wrong, do not repay him with a wrong. Try to do what everyone considers to be good. Do everything possible on your part to live in peace with everybody. Never take revenge, my friends, but instead let God's anger do it. For the scripture says, "I will take revenge, I will pay back, says the Lord." Instead, as the scripture says: "If your enemies are hungry, feed them; if they are thirsty, give them a drink; for by doing this you will make them burn with shame." Do not let evil defeat you; instead, conquer evil with good. (Romans 12:19–21; see also Exodus 23:4–5)

When wrongs tempt us to vengeance, we must say with Joseph, "Am I in the place of God?"

Some angry people in our day cry, "No justice, no peace." God certainly tells his people to do justice when it is within their power (Micah 6:8). He permits self-defense. But not revenge. If we refuse to live in peace when we have suffered injustice, there will never be peace, because in this age, before God's final day of judgment, injustices will never end. God made and redeemed us for love and mercy, not vengeance. The slogan, "No justice, no peace" is powerful, but not for good. God has given civil authorities the duty of punishing evil (Romans 13:1–7). They often do it badly. But when injustice tempts us to take matters into our own hands, we should stop and say with Joseph, "Am I in the place of God?"

Jesus knew that pious people would one day want to give his disciples special honors. He criticized the scribes and Pharisees for enjoying being called "Father" and being greeted respectfully as "Teacher." His disciples would face the same eagerness from people to do the same. So Jesus continued,

> You must not be called "Teacher," because you are all members of one family and have only one Teacher. And you must not call anyone here on earth "Father," because you have only the one Father in heaven. Nor should you be called "Leader," because your one and only leader is the Messiah. The greatest one among you must be your servant. (Matthew 23:8–11)

In the civil realm, Christians give honor where it is due (Romans 13:7; 1 Peter 2:17). Likewise, elders deserve honor (Hebrews 13:7; 1 Thessalonians 5:12). Jesus, however, makes a distinction between the honor that civil leaders enjoy and how his followers are to behave.

> You know that the rulers of the heathen have power over them, and the leaders have complete authority. This, however, is not the way it shall be among you. If one of you wants to be great, he must be the servant of the rest; and if one of you wants to be first, he must be your slave—like the Son of Man, who did not come to be served, but to serve and to give his life to redeem many people. (Matthew 20:25–28)

In the Book of Acts, Paul is simply called Paul, and Peter is Peter. They were apostles with an apostle's authority, but no one addressed them as "Apostle Paul," "Reverend

Peter," or, even worse, "Apostle." There is no evidence that the apostles or elders were called "Father," "Leader," "Reverend," or "Pastor."

During my last five years teaching high school, my students, especially my calculus students, began calling me "Dr. Edgar," even though I always introduced myself as "Mr. Edgar." At first, I did not like the reverential tone they used, but then I found myself rather enjoying it. Better I should have said firmly, "I am an adult and a teacher like any other teacher. Just call me Mr. Edgar."

Whenever God gives a person success, he should say thank you to God for building his house (Psalm 127:1). And when someone begins, however obliquely, to credit someone with godlike status, the answer should be swift and determined: "Am I in the place of God?" Any other answer tempts the hearer to walk the snake's path, with its promise, "You shall be as God."

Protestants end the prayer Jesus taught us to pray with, "For yours is the kingdom, and the power, and the glory forever." The glory of reverential address in his church belongs to God alone. The right of vengeance belongs to God alone. And God reserves to himself the power of blessing us with children and working with success. "Except the LORD build the house, they labor in vain that build it." Am I in the place of God? God forbid!

Our first four questions are from the Bible's first book, Genesis. Our next question is the New Testament's first question. But before listening to it, we must look at the rest of the Old Testament, which tells the history of Israel, the nation that came from Abraham.

THE STORY OF
ISRAEL FROM JOSEPH TO JESUS'S BIRTH

"OI! TEN THOUSAND years will give you such a crick in the neck!" complained the Genie, oozing from the lamp in the movie *Aladdin*. While it's a mere two thousand years from the end of Genesis, the Old Testament's first book, to Matthew, the New Testament's first book, a lot of notable events took place. When Joseph lived, the Rome that ruled the world when Jesus was born did not yet exist.

More appears in those two thousand years than the Ark of the Covenant that Indiana Jones searched for, or the shepherd David who unexpectedly kills the Philistine giant Goliath, or the beautiful poems like Psalm 23. We fly like a bird from Joseph in Egypt to the New Testament's first question, watching empires appear and disappear, heroes and villains fight, and two new covenants that God made, first with Israel and then with David.

After Joseph brought Israel's family to Egypt—Israel is Jacob's other name—they lived there 400 years. Growing to be a large nation, they frightened the Egyptians, who made them slaves and then used male infanticide to limit their numbers (Exodus 1). Finally, God sent a savior named Moses, defeated the gods and armies of Egypt, and rescued Israel. To this day, Jews celebrate their deliverance with the Feast of Passover.

God led Israel to Mount Sinai, where he made a covenant with them, a multi-part treaty God himself wrote— no negotiations! It included past history ("I am the LORD your God who brought you out of Egypt, where you were slaves" [Exodus 20:2]), rules for Israel to obey, blessings for obedience, curses for disobedience, and the sign of circumcision. Its heart was God's promise: "I will be your God and you will be my People" (Exodus 6:7; 29:45; Leviticus 26:45; 2 Corinthians 6:16; Revelation 21:7). Covenant rules included: 1) God's eternal moral law, the Ten Commandments written on stone and placed in the Ark of the Covenant, 2) his temporary rules for worship with animal sacrifices, feast days, priests and Levites, a worship tent, and rules for ritual cleanliness, and 3) civil laws for Israel (Books of Exodus–Deuteronomy). When it was time, God directed Israel to confirm the covenant by animal sacrifice (Exodus 24:8; see Luke 22:20).

After leaving Mount Sinai, Israel wandered for forty years, until Joshua led them in conquering Canaan, the land God had promised to Abraham. Joshua divided the land among Israel's twelve tribes (Books of Numbers and Joshua). For the next 400 years, Israel did the same thing over and over. First, they obeyed God and prospered;

next they followed other gods and God punished them by means of enemy nations; third, they returned to God, repented, and asked God to save them; fourth, God heard them and sent memorable Judges like Gideon and Samson to fight their enemies. Eventually, each man did whatever he wanted to. Life became horrible in anarchic Israel (Book of Judges).

Israel's last judge was Samuel, the first of the prophets. The people asked him for a king like other nations had, and God gave them Saul. For forty years, King Saul did great things but in the end he failed because his heart was not right with God. About the year 1000 B.C., God gave the kingdom to David from the tribe of Judah. He was a great warrior, a musician, and a poet. Although David became Saul's son-in-law, jealous Saul tried to kill him. David escaped, and finally took the throne after Saul died in battle with the Philistines. Although a badly flawed man himself, David was a man after God's own heart, and God promised him in a covenant that his dynasty would rule forever (Books 1 Samuel–2 Samuel).

David's successors repeated the history of the time of the Judges. David's son Solomon built a magnificent temple for God in Jerusalem, but in his old age he foolishly built temples for his idolatrous foreign wives. God therefore divided Solomon's kingdom into two: a northern kingdom of ten tribes called Israel, and a southern one called Judah. Despite the heroic work of the prophets Elijah and Elisha, wicked rulers like King Ahab and Queen Jezebel finally made Israel so evil that God said, "Time's up," and in 722 B.C. sent Israel into captivity in Assyria.

In Judah, the Davidic kings were a mixed lot, leading Judah from the living God to idols and back again. Finally, when Judah sacrificed their own children to other gods, and worshiped the sun, moon, and stars, God sent them into captivity in Babylon. Babylon's great king Nebuchadnezzar conquered Jerusalem in 587 B.C., tore down its walls, destroyed Solomon's temple, and left the city empty (Books 1 Kings–2 Chronicles, Isaiah, Jeremiah, Lamentations, Ezekiel, and Daniel).

Just before Jerusalem was conquered, the prophet Ezekiel, already in Babylon, saw God leave the temple (Ezekiel 10). At the same time in Jerusalem, Jeremiah prophesied that after seventy years God would bring the Jews—their name taken from Judah —back to Jerusalem and give them a new covenant to replace the old one given at Mount Sinai (Jeremiah 25; 31). Jeremiah prophesied that, unlikely as it seemed in defeat and exile, God would keep his covenant with David: one of his sons would always be king (Jeremiah 33).

Great as Babylon was, it did not last. The Persians conquered it in 539 B.C., and King Cyrus sent about 50,000 Jews back to Jerusalem to re-found the city and build a temple (Books of Ezra and Nehemiah). The returned Jews did not really want to build a temple, but God sent prophets to urge them on, with promises of a coming son of David who by his presence would make the new temple glorious (Books of Haggai and Zechariah).

Finally, God sent the Jews one more prophet, Malachi, whose book closes the Old Testament. Through Malachi, God said, "I will send my messenger to prepare the way for me. Then the Lord you are looking for will suddenly come to his Temple. The messenger you long to see will come and proclaim my covenant" (Malachi 3:1). God's saving power would rise on his people "like the sun and bring healing like the sun's rays" (Malachi 4:2). The Christmas carol "Hark! The Herald Angels Sing" quotes Malachi in its third verse:

Hail the Heav'n-born Prince of Peace!
  Hail the Sun of Righteousness!
Light and life to all He brings,
  Ris'n with healing in His wings.

Then the Jews waited another 400 years for a son of David to come and save them.

What happened in these 400 years? First, Alexander the Great with his Macedonian and Greek army conquered Persia. After his death, two of his Greek generals founded dynasties in Syria and Egypt that fought back and forth to control Palestine (named for the Philistines) that lay between them. At length in 160 B.C. a family of Jewish heroes called the Maccabees led Israel in a fight for independence against the Syrian Greeks. The Maccabees were a priestly family, from the tribe of Levi, so they could not be David's heirs. The Feast of Hanukkah commemorates how Temple worship began again after their victory.

In 63 B.C. Antony took over Palestine for Rome, and Caesar Augustus later allowed Herod the Great to rule Palestine on behalf of Rome. The Jews acknowledged Rome's supremacy by paying taxes and putting up with Roman soldiers. By Herod's time, the Jews had grown to nation size again, spreading from Judea around Jerusalem, across the Jordan River to the east, and north into Galilee. There were Jewish settlements in all of the great cities of the Roman Empire, where Jews gathered in their synagogues each Sabbath to pray and to read from Moses's Law, the Prophets, and the Psalms.

When Jesus was born, the Jewish hopes and prayers for a coming son of David to be their savior did not include all that the prophets had foretold. They missed the meaning of Psalms 22 and 110, the suffering servant of Isaiah 53, and the rejected shepherd king of Zechariah 9–14. Neither did they anticipate that God would send a prophet like Moses who would bring a new covenant (Deuteronomy 18:15–19; Jeremiah 31:31–34). What they wanted was another Maccabean hero to lead them in a war of national liberation against Rome. So they gave their sons Maccabean names, such as Matthew, Simon, John, and Judas, names common in the New Testament, and they gave their daughters names like Mary, prominent in the Hasmonean (Maccabean) dynasty.

When Jesus was born, therefore, Augustus was Caesar, the Emperor of Rome, and there was peace after a series of civil wars. So, "when the right time finally came, God sent his own Son. He came as the son of a human mother and lived under the Jewish Law" (Galatians 4:4).

5

ASTROLOGERS

"WHERE IS THE BABY BORN TO BE KING OF THE JEWS"

MATTHEW 2:1-12

AT CHRISTMAS TIME in our neighborhood people festoon their houses and yards with lights. Families set up trees inside their houses and decorate them. People buy gifts, and the music on the radio changes. Schools take a break. And nativity scenes go up, depicting baby Jesus in an animal food trough (manger). His family, some shepherds, and animals in a small barn surround him. The scene also includes three men in strange clothes, often with crowns on their heads, each with a gift for the baby. Above the tableau is a star.

These three men in the nativity scene had seen a remarkable star and followed it to Jerusalem where they asked the New Testament's first question. "Where is the baby born to be the king of the Jews? We saw his star when it came up in the east, and we have come to worship him" (Matthew 2:2).

The men were Magi, considered by Romans as evil magicians (the word "magi" is translated as "magician" in Acts 8:8; 13:8). But people in the east (likely Persia) respected them as wise men because they practiced astrology and claimed to know the course of human affairs from the stars. Seeing a star—one they interpreted as a sign that a new king of the Jews had been born—they followed it to worship this King. Maybe, since Jews had lived in Persia for centuries, these men knew Balaam's prophecy relating a star and an important king of the Jews (Numbers 24:15–19).

The Magi's journey to find the King took them to Herod the Great, whom the Roman Senate had made "King of the Jews." King Herod was a great builder, most notably making the Second Temple spectacular. He was also a paranoid murderer who killed his father-in-law, two sons, and two wives. Not surprisingly, Herod was furious to hear that a new King of the Jews had been born. He knew the prophecies foretelling the birth of a Jewish King (in Hebrew "Messiah," that is, "Anointed One," and "Christ" in Greek) so he asked his Bible experts where the Christ would be born. They replied, "the prophet wrote: 'Bethlehem in the land of Judah...from you will come a leader who will guide my people Israel'"(Matthew 2:5; Micah 5:2).

Crafty old Herod told the Magi to go to Bethlehem to

find the baby, and then come back to tell Herod where the baby was so that he too could worship him. God, however, thwarted Herod's plan to kill the baby and sent the Magi a dream warning them to go home another way. When Herod saw he had been tricked, the enraged old man sent his soldiers to kill every baby boy in Bethlehem two years old and younger. But by then Jesus, with his mother Mary and her husband Joseph, had already escaped to Egypt, sent there by God in a dream he gave to Joseph.

Why was the newborn King of the Jews so important that Magi came seeking him and Herod tried to kill him? As the King of the Jews, he fulfilled God's promise to David to provide an heir to his throne (2 Samuel 7:13; Isaiah 11:1). His identity as David's son is both the first and last thing the New Testament says about him (Matthew 1:1; Revelation 22:16), and it was the charge under which Pontius Pilate had him crucified (Luke 23:38).

But while faithful Jews waited for their Messiah as a political savior, they completely missed the fullness of God's salvation in two ways. First, in Jesus, God took human flesh to dwell with his people (Exodus 29:45; 1 Kings 6:13; Zechariah 2:10; John 1:14) and save them from sin and death, not by triumphing in battle but by dying sacrificially on a cross (Isaiah 53). That's why an angel told Joseph in a dream to name Mary's son "Jesus—because he will save his people from their sins" (Matthew 1:21).

Second, the Jews missed how their Messiah's kingdom would include all nations, not by conquest, but by calling them to turn from their idolatry and instead worship the Living God revealed in Jesus. In that way, God's kingdom would grow to cover the whole earth and include all nations (Daniel 2:34–35; Zechariah 2:11; Psalm 22:31; Romans 1:16; Luke 24:47; Acts 1:8).

People everywhere know that something fundamental is wrong with the world and are ready to follow any leader who promises to fix things (Matthew 24:5). After World War I, Germany longed for a savior, and hailed and obeyed Adolph Hitler, who promised them salvation and greatness. After Communist armies conquered China, millions of Chinese soon read Chairman Mao's Little Red Book, hoping to find within it China's salvation. However, everyone who trusts human politicians to set the world right side up will be disappointed. Kings and presidents are mere men and sinners themselves, so God tells us not to trust in them (Psalm 146:3). The true savior has already come. He is Jesus, the King of the Jews and the desire of the nations (Haggai 2:7).

Christians have often evaded the fact that our savior is Jewish, portraying him, for example, as a blond, blue-eyed northern European, and even hating Jews. A popular short summary of the Bible—"Creation, Fall, Redemption, Consummation"—leaves out Israel and thereby most of the Old Testament, its prophecies, its wisdom, its heroes, and how God chose Israel as a light to the nations. Jesus, King of the Jews, is that light! How appropriately we put up lights at Christmas time. How appropriately the Magi saw the light of a star and followed it to Bethlehem!

The arrival of the Magi signified the beginning of the nations repenting and turning to God in Christ (Acts 17:30–31). The most significant development in human history for the last two thousand years is not the fall of Rome, nor the printing press, nor Science and Enlightenment, nor the Industrial Revolution, nor democratic government, nor the promise of socialist justice, nor European imperialism and its retreat, nor huge population growth, nor the computer and the Internet, nor climate change. The greatest and best thing is the continuing spread of the knowledge of the Living God through Jesus, the King of the Jews, who now sends his followers out from Jerusalem, just as the Magi once came there to worship him (Matthew 28:18–20). The messengers from Jesus—missionaries—bring a gift to the nations that they were not looking for (Isaiah 65:1; Romans 10:20).

I once had three calculus classes who had had all the right teachers before me, so I did not have to teach them algebra, geometry, or trigonometry, just calculus. It was wonderful. I thought and thought how to say thank you to their previous math teachers, but came up with no good idea. Finally, on the day of our annual math department Christmas party, I knew what to do: give them a gift they never imagined getting. I had sixty calculus students each write a thank-you note to each of their three previous math teachers, asked my wife to get folders for them, and brought them out at gift exchange time. One student asked, "Are they really going to care?" "Oh my, yes!" I said. "By the time we open presents, many will have drunk too much, and we'll be loud and boisterous, but when they get these notes, they will immediately fall silent and read them." And that is exactly what happened when these public high school teachers got a gift they were not looking for. Years later, one told me it was the best Christmas present she had ever gotten. Another turned to them when a wolf pack of parents attacked her one year as a horrible teacher. (She was merely insisting that their ninth-grade children actually learn something!) So it is when people receive the gift from God who sent his Son to die for them. They know they have a treasure (Matthew 13:44–46).

Today, we look back over two thousand years and see how others have followed the three Magi and bowed to Jesus: Greeks and Romans whom the Jews despised, northern barbarians whom the Greeks long scorned, and in the last two centuries the Africans and Asians whom Europeans looked down on. And in all times and places, lowly shepherds, women, and slaves have found salvation and dignity in Jesus (Galatians 3:28; Colossians 3:11).

Next Christmas, when you see a nativity scene, look at the three Magi and remember their question, "Where is the baby born to be the king of the Jews? We saw his star when it came up in the east, and we have come to worship him." Then think, "Those astrologers represent *me*. The King of the Jews, who died for their sins, died for mine also, so that 'Everyone who calls on the name of the Lord will be saved'" (Romans 10:13; Acts 2:21).

6

JESUS

"DO YOU WANT TO BE HEALED"

?

JOHN 5:2-17

WHEN I TAUGHT mathematics, my Algebra II students would get angry when we got to imaginary numbers. They rebelled against the very term "*Imaginary* Number!" They also knew that, once again, math teachers had been lying to them for years: "You can't take the square root of a negative number." And, now, just like that, you can take the square root of a negative number just by calling the result an *imaginary* number.

Schools regularly lie to students. "You can be anything you want to be." Completely untrue! "There is no such thing as a stupid question." Here's one: A teacher told a class how his uncle had died when a Canada goose flew into his windshield on the Pennsylvania turnpike. Up goes a hand: "There's one thing I don't get about what happened to your uncle. How did a Canada goose get to Pennsylvania?"

At the Bethesda Pool in Jerusalem, Jesus asked a man who had been crippled and unable to walk for thirty-eight years, "Do you want to be healed?" It sounds like a stupid question. Was it?

The Pool of Bethesda in Jerusalem, near the temple, was a trapezoid with bases of 220 and 165 feet and a height of 315 feet. A bridge bisected the trapezoid. The roofed colonnades along each side and over the bridge made five colonnades in all where people could sit and beg. The blind, the lame, and the paralyzed sat under these colonnades daily, hoping to be the first in the water when it bubbled up and thereby be healed.

From the multitude of invalids, Jesus chose one, a middle-aged beggar, and asked him, "Do you want to be healed?" It was not in fact a stupid question. Here is what the man would lose if he were healed: He would lose long-time friends, both those he regularly begged with and regular givers. He would have to start working, probably as a day laborer, waiting every morning with other landless men to see if someone would hire him. So he might not really want to be healed, since being able to walk would create new problems for him.

Jesus could ask every troubled soul the same question: "Do you want to be healed?" Former Philadelphia basketball star Charles Barkley said in a TV interview I watched that he had grown up without his father and never heard from him. Then one day, he got a call: "Hi. I'm your father. Can you get me tickets for tonight's game?" That request would make any young man angry. Did Charles want to be healed of his anger? Eventually, he decided that his father was the only father he would ever have, so he should make the best of it. A young man visited me. He was sick of living a double life: church on Sunday and gay bookstores during the week. "Do you want to stop with the bookstores?" I asked. "Yes." An old woman I knew recited eighty-year-old grudges against her long dead father. Did she want to live grudge free? Actually, no! Name any spiritual, emotional, or physical ill handicapping you, and "Do you want to be healed?" becomes a profound question.

Here is how the man reacted to Jesus's question. First, he looked up at Jesus, a stranger. Most beggars sit with their heads bowed, droning on asking for money. Second, he replied, "Sir, I have no one here to put me in the pool when the water is stirred up; while I am trying to get in, somebody else gets there first" (John 5:7). There was the answer to Jesus's question: yes, he did want to be healed. Jesus then gave the man a command that surely sounded cruel to anyone hearing him: "Get up, pick up your mat, and walk" (John 5:8). Jesus did not invite him to obey; he commanded him, just as he commanded his first disciples, "Follow me."

What would a crippled man think when a stranger commanded him to get up, pick up his mat, and walk? Perhaps, "Impossible. I can't stand up, and he knows that! Why else would I sit here every day? What I want is help to get into the water when it bubbles." But instead this man tried to stand, and his legs worked. Did he try confidently, full of faith in this stranger who spoke with such authority? Or did he think, "Oh, whatever! Might as well try?" In any case, he tried, and Jesus healed him. He stood up, picked up his mat, and walked away from the Pool of Bethesda. He had just enough trust in Jesus to try to obey, and Jesus did not let him down.

Here is the main point about faith: Where is it placed? Once there were two men traveling together, one confident and the other one fearful. They came to a deep ravine they had to cross. Right ahead was an old bridge made of decaying rope and wood slats. The confident traveler walked out on it, and it broke. He tumbled to his death far below. His fearful companion walked a quarter mile up the ravine to a new steel and concrete bridge. Trembling with fear, he edged himself along it and arrived safely to the other side. His faith was weak, but he was on the right bridge. Even weak faith in Jesus saves, while the strongest faith in anyone or anything else will not save.

So what was life like for this newly healed man? Not so good. As he was carrying his mat through the streets of Jerusalem, some Jewish authorities stopped him. "You can't do that on the Sabbath Day!" He answered, "The man who healed me told me to carry my bed." "Who was that?" they asked, rather than asking the more obvious question, "You were crippled and now you can walk? How did that happen?" The newly healed man answered that he did not know who healed him. Evidently, he had not asked Jesus his name, and probably he had not thanked him either.

Going on to the temple, the healed man suddenly found himself facing Jesus again, who said, "Listen, you are well now; so stop sinning or something worse may happen to you" (John 5:14). Right away, this nameless man ran to the Jewish authorities to report that a man named Jesus had healed him. So Jesus was now in trouble for healing on the Sabbath Day, and his enemies wanted to kill him.

All in all, this cripple whom Jesus healed is not an attractive person. Why Jesus chose him out of all the invalids sitting around the pool is a mystery rooted in God's eternal plan. There are, in fact, no worthy people whom the Lord chooses to save, any more than Israel was a worthy nation to be chosen (Deuteronomy 7:7; 9:5; Romans 3:23).

Do you want to be healed, or do you like your grudges, your porn, your pride, or your anger? If you are tired of your slavery to sin, then look toward Jesus and do what he commands. What is that? "The right time has come," Jesus said when he began preaching, "and the kingdom of God is near! Turn away from your sins and believe the Good News!" (Mark 1:15). "What God wants you to do is believe in the one he sent," namely Jesus (John 6:29). As the sign of belonging to him, Jesus's followers are baptized in his name and added to his church, where believers gather to worship him each Sunday (Matthew 28:18–20). Believe in Jesus, repent of sin, and believe the good announcement about who Jesus is and what he did.

The Bible's Good Story (gospel) is that Jesus is David's heir, God come in the flesh, born of a woman to be the Lamb of God, who crushed the snake's head, and defeated sin and death by rising from his tomb to sit enthroned at God's right hand in heaven. Jesus now rules all nations and will soon come, when everyone will stand before him as their judge (Acts 17:31).

As Jesus said with kingly authority to the crippled man, "Stand, pick up your mat, and go home," so he says with kingly authority to everyone who hears him, "Believe in me, and you will be saved. Come and follow me." Then your life of obedience and adventure will begin, extending on into eternity.

Jesus asks everyone who hears him, "Do you want to be healed?" It is not a stupid question at all, but a profound one. That question searches our hearts, asking, "Do you want to be saved? Are you ready to give up the sins that you love and follow Jesus? Then get up and do it!"

ANGEL

"WHY ARE YOU LOOKING AMONG THE DEAD FOR ONE WHO IS ALIVE"

MATTHEW 27:55–28:8; MARK 15:47–16:8; LUKE 23:50–24:11; JOHN 20:1

PEOPLE OFTEN LOOK for what they want in the wrong place. I once had a student who finished a math test and then erased his correct answers to copy his neighbor's wrong ones. Eve and Adam wanted to be wise and followed the snake's advice to eat fruit from a tree God had forbidden and became foolish instead (Genesis 3:6-7; see Romans 1:21-23). After Jesus was buried, loyal women who loved him went looking for his body in the wrong place, his grave.

Angels met them with a rebuke: You are looking in the wrong place. Here is what happened.

Jewish rulers who hated Jesus got Roman soldiers and Temple guards to arrest Jesus at night when he was alone with his disciples. All the disciples fled. Before the Jews' highest court, the Sanhedrin, the high priest put Jesus on oath, asking him, "Are you the Messiah, the Son of the Blessed One?" (Mark 14:61) "I am," answered Jesus, "and you will all see the Son of Man seated at the right side of the Almighty and coming with the clouds of heaven!" (Mark 14:62; see Daniel 7:13 and Psalm 110:1). Immediately the court convicted Jesus of blasphemy.

In the morning they took Jesus to Pilate, the Roman governor, and falsely told him that Jesus was plotting rebellion against Caesar. After a short trial, Pilate declared Jesus to be innocent. Nevertheless, Pilate ordered his soldiers to scourge Jesus and then crucify him in order to satisfy the Jewish leaders.

So at Passover, when Jews remembered God's saving them from slavery in Egypt and sacrificed a lamb, Jesus, "the Lamb of God who takes away the sin of the world" died (John 1:29). He crushed the head of the snake that asked Eve, "Did God really say?" He fulfilled the meaning of the ram that Abraham sacrificed instead of his son Isaac. In fact, wherever the story of Jesus's sacrifice is told, animal sacrifices soon cease. The news about the sacrifice of Jesus for sin makes them now meaningless.

Jesus was buried hurriedly late on a Friday afternoon on a shelf in the rock tomb that Joseph from Arimathea, a rich man, owned. Another rich man, Nicodemus, provided some spices for a quick burial before sundown, the start of the Jewish Sabbath day of rest.

After the Sabbath rest, on the first day of the week,

some women who had followed Jesus from Galilee to Jerusalem and had watched him die, headed towards his tomb with spices to complete his burial. With birds singing, trees covered with new leaves, and flowers perfuming the air, they went to the tomb. Combining the different Gospel accounts, it seems likely that there were five women, three of whom were named Mary: Mary from the village of Magdala; Mary, Jesus's mother; Mary, the mother of James; Joanna, the wife of Chuza, King Herod's steward; and Salome, perhaps the mother of James and John.

For two reasons women rather than men came to finish burying Jesus. First, preparing bodies for burial was considered women's work at the time. Second, the men were hiding. As Jesus had prophesied, the disciples had scattered: "Strike the shepherd, and the sheep will be scattered" (Matthew 26:31; quoting Zechariah 13:7).

"Sheep without a shepherd" is an ancient picture of people with no leader or protector. Few people today have seen a flock of sheep with or without a shepherd, so "sheep scattered" only vaguely tells us how the women felt. Here is my story of how they felt: Two boys, ages five and six, wake up on a Saturday morning, February 14, 1953—Valentine's Day—and run into Mother's room. "How's Daddy?" they asked. They knew he was in the hospital, but they had barely understood that his remaining kidney was failing. Mother answers, "Daddy's dead," and bursts into tears, burying her face in her hands. Daddy—who gave us love and security, who made life fun—was dead. We crept from the room, feeling guilty for making Mother cry. We were alone for the rest of the day: Mother had to deal with the hospital, the funeral home, and the cemetery. The next day was lonelier. At church, two old women told me separately: "Now *you* have to be the man of the house," a burden a six-year-old boy can no more bear than carry an elephant. Sheep without a shepherd, the newly fatherless and the widowed—such were these women.

As the women walked, they pondered a practical problem: Who would roll away the stone, a giant disk, six feet or so in diameter, perhaps six inches thick, set in stone grooves? They would have to roll it uphill like a tire and then wedge a stone in front of it. They were not strong enough to do that.

Then the earth shook under their feet. An angel rolled back the stone and sat on it as they approached the tomb. He looked like lightning, and his clothes were white as snow. The Roman soldiers guarding the tomb, scared witless, fell on their faces. So when the women got to the tomb, the stone was rolled away. Inside it, they met two angels. Like the soldiers, the women also fell to the ground. An angel asked, "Why are you looking among the dead for one who is alive? He is not here. He has been raised" (Luke 24:5).

As we think about the women going to Jesus's tomb, we sympathize with their devastating despair and their love for Jesus. But the angel rebuked them for coming to the tomb. "Remember what he said to you while he was in Galilee: 'The Son of Man must be handed over to sinners, be crucified, and three days later rise to life.' Then the women remembered his words" (Luke 24:6–8). Running from the tomb, they hurried to the hiding men and told them that the tomb was empty and what the angel had said. Peter and John ran to the tomb and confirmed their news: it was empty (John 20:1–8).

Notice four things here. First, the four Gospels do not tell exactly the same story. It is like when you talk to crime witnesses who have not been allowed to speak with each other: each usually tells the truth, but emphasizes something different. It is the identical story from witnesses that detectives don't trust. Similarly, get five people to report on the same meeting, and you will get five versions of the meeting, all true, but never identical.

Second, it was all women who found the tomb empty. Someone making up the story would have been strongly inclined to make prominent men like Joseph and Nicodemus the witnesses, not women. But the Gospel writers told the story as it happened.

Third, the guards eventually got up and ran off to the Jewish leaders, who paid them to say that the disciples stole the body (Matthew 28:11–15). Really? The frightened disciples—who ran when Jesus was arrested—overpowered Roman soldiers, moved the stone, stole the body, and talked the women into telling a story about an earthquake, angels, and a message? The only plausible part of this story is the male disciples moving the stone.

Fourth, as in all eyewitness accounts, the central story in Matthew, Mark, Luke, and John is consistent: women came early in the morning with spices for Jesus's body; there was an earthquake; an angel rolled away the stone; the tomb was empty; and an angel asked, "Why are you looking among the dead for one who is alive?"

They were searching for the living among the dead because of unbelief. They did not believe Jesus, who healed the sick, stilled a storm at sea, gave sight to the blind, walked on water, raised the dead to life, and fed five thousand people with five loaves and two fish. They did not believe him when he said he would be killed and on the third day rise from the dead.

When people disbelieve God's Word, they look for life in a world cursed to futility and decay, but cannot find it there. Apart from God, every strategy people use to find life fails. Will you look for life and meaning in building and creating? When you are done, you won't find it satisfying. Try going for experiences—travel, drugs, sex, or skydiving. It will leave you empty. Gather a lot of wealth. You'll have to leave it behind to someone else, maybe a fool. Become wise? That beats being a fool, but in the end, the wise and the fool both die. Live a thousand years, have a hundred children, get rich, and still it will end badly. Death wins. Under the sun, apart from God, it's all smoke and mirrors.

I ended my last day as a high school teacher by proctoring students taking an English exam. At its end, their old teacher came in to say goodbye. He looked at them, shook his head, and said, "Vanity of vanities, all is vanity" (Ecclesiastes 1:2).

"Of the making of many books there is no end," I answered (Ecclesiastes 12:12).

"There is nothing new under the sun," he said (Ecclesiastes 1:9).

"Here is the conclusion: fear God and keep his commandments, for this is the whole duty of man," I replied (Ecclesiastes 12:13).

And we dismissed the students with him saying once more, "Vanity of vanities, all is vanity." The students left, no doubt thinking we were two old men who had lost our wits. Apart from God, death reigns, and unbelief can do no better than look for life in the ruins of a sin-devastated world.

What is wrong with the human race? Our worst fault is that we won't fear God or believe him. That was the women's fault. They had not believed Jesus when he said he would rise from death, so they went to his tomb. Yes, they loved Jesus and wanted to do right. But no, they did not believe him, so they looked for the living among the dead.

Where do you look for life? Parents, teachers,

politicians, and bloggers tell young people to pursue their dreams. What dreams? Successful careers. Happy families. Great experiences. "Making a difference." Building something! They utter idiocies like, "Believe in yourself," or, like the windbag Polonius in Shakespeare's play *Hamlet*, "To thine own self be true."

Old people sometimes tell the young, "Life is short," or that at seventy-five no one will care if you were once CEO of a company. But young people don't believe the old because they don't believe Jesus, who said that a full life belongs to the poor in spirit, to the humble before God and man, to the peacemakers, and yes, even to the persecuted (Matthew 5:1–11). They don't believe Jesus who said, "Don't bother getting rich on earth. It won't last," and "Don't worry about tomorrow" (Matthew 6:19–21; 25–34).

And you know what? Old people don't believe Jesus either. So people keep on looking for the living among the dead, not believing Jesus that in him alone there is life.

In my life, I have worked with many good people, traveled far, helped to raise a family, and enjoyed many good things. I can point to a few worthwhile things I have done. But where is *life*? After I die, no one will long remember me or what I have done. Only Jesus has life, and he is my judge. You will never hear sweeter words than these: "Well done, good and faithful servant. Enter into the joy of your Lord," nor worse words than these, "Depart from me you workers of iniquity, for I do not know you" (Matthew 25:23; 7:21–23). Believe Jesus. Live to hear these words, and you will not be caught looking for the living among the dead. Only the Lord Jesus Christ has conquered death, and all who are united to him by faith and trust in him will live also.

Slandered and murdered by his enemies, Jesus died and then returned to life. His resurrection changes everything.

It dispels the gloom of life, which always ends in death. One might say to everyone born of woman, "Abandon hope, all ye who enter life," because death awaits you. But one can't say that to Christians. They have stopped looking for the living among the dead.

On Easter morning, Greeks use a special greeting, "Christos aneste!" (Christ is risen!) The reply is, "Alethos aneste." (He is risen indeed!) In the now dissolved Soviet Union that ruled the former Russian Empire, the Communist Party conducted campaigns from time to time to teach "scientific atheism." In one village, the commissar called everyone, including the priest, together in front of the church, and talked for an hour about the illusions of religion. Then he magnanimously motioned to the priest, saying, "You may have five minutes to answer me." "I do not need five minutes," the priest said, and, turning to his villagers, he said, "He is risen!" With one voice, they responded, "He is risen indeed" (Peter Berger, *First Things*, April 2016, p. 42). Those words refute all atheism, all despair, all selfishness, and all vain seeking for life and meaning in a world that is passing away.

Jesus is alive, so like the five women who in unbelief went looking for the living among the dead but instead found life, we testify with them the best announcement the world has ever heard: Jesus, the King of the Jews, died for our sins according to the Scriptures, and then, according to his own word, he rose from the dead, to be seen alive by many people. He lives to save all who worship him with Thomas's words, "My Lord and my God" (John 20:28). We do not need to search for the living among the dead. We live and we die expecting to meet Jesus at his coming, when we will stand again on this earth with him. There are no fatherless Christians. The Lord is our living Shepherd.

QUESTIONS FOR DISCUSSION

1

Snake: Did God Really Say?

1. How did the snake offer the woman a "declaration of independence?"

2. When have you seen people fall for the insinuating question, "Did God really say?"

3. The fruit from the tree God forbade tasted good. What things can you think of that feel good but God does not allow?

4. Read Genesis 3:10–13. How did the relationship between the first man and woman change after each ate the fruit?

5. Read Genesis 3:14–24. In what ways besides childbirth itself do children bring pain to their mothers? See also Proverbs 10:1, 15:20, 17:25, 29:15.

6. What are some implications of God's curse of the ground for our work and the earth?

7. How does knowing that yes, you too will die affect how you live?

2

God: Where Are You?

1. Compare the examples below with God's question to the first man and woman. How did God call each one?

   a. Elijah: 1 Kings 19:1–18

   b. Saul: 1 Samuel 10

   c. Sheep and Coin: Luke 15:1–10

   d. Zacchaeus: Luke 19:1–10

2. When and how have you heard God calling, "Where are you?" Write your spiritual autobiography of when God called, "Where are you?"

3. How might you communicate God's question of "Where are you?" to a relative or neighbor?

4. Read Matthew 7:6, 10:14; Acts 28:17–29; 1 Peter 3:1. What does God tell believers to do if people refuse to listen to them talk about God?

3

Isaac: Where Is the Lamb?

1. Animal sacrifice was nearly universal in ancient civilizations. Why do you think it was so common?

2. How could some ancient civilizations sacrifice children to their gods? Do modern people do anything similar?

3. Did Abraham lie to Isaac when he told him, "God will provide"? Explain your yes or no.

4. How do Genesis 1:28, 3:15, 15:5, and 21:2 and Matthew 1:21 relate to each other?

5. "Indeed...sins are forgiven only if blood is poured out" (Hebrews 9:22). Why is blood so necessary for sin to be forgiven?

6. Read Luke 9:23; Romans 12:1; Philippians 2:7, 4:18; Hebrews 13:15–16; and 1 Peter 2:5. Animal sacrifice loses

its meaning for people who know about Jesus. How do his followers still sacrifice?

7. In what ways do people who reject Jesus's death on their behalf try to deal with their guilt?

4

Jacob and Joseph: Am I in the Place of God?

1. The first verb in the Bible is "created" (Genesis 1:1). What creatures does the first chapter of Genesis name?

2. What is the basic thing you have in common with the sun, lions, and turnips?

3. Has anyone ever tried to speak to you as though you had godlike power, intelligence, authority, or honor? What did you do? What should you have done?

4. Protestants criticize the Roman Catholic Church for calling their priests "Father." Have Protestant churches fallen into a similar error? How?

5. In what ways are scientists and others today trying to "play God"?

6. Which of the Ten Commandments deals with the difference between the Creator and his creatures?

7. What does God mean when he calls himself a "jealous God"?

5

Astrologers: Where Is the Baby Born to Be King of the Jews?

1. Why does Christian tradition think of exactly three astrologers?

2. Read Deuteronomy 18:10–14 and Exodus 20:3. Do you or your friends check your horoscopes? How harmless or dangerous is this practice?

3. Can you think of times when you were involved in something quite wrong and through that experience God showed you truth about him? What was that truth?

4. What connection might there be between Malachi 4:2 and the astrologers' arrival from the east?

5. How important is it that the New Testament opens and closes with telling us that Jesus is the Son of David (Matthew 1:1; Revelation 22:16)? How is that fact important to you when you think about Jesus?

6. Why have Christians sometimes ignored, or even forgotten, that their King Jesus is Jewish?

7. How can Jesus be both King of the Jews and the Lamb of God?

6

Jesus: Do You Want to Be Healed?

1. Why did the crippled man not recognize Jesus, let alone know his name?

2. Jesus chose to approach and heal one man at the Pool of Bethesda, bypassing hundreds of others. How come?

3. What does Jesus's choice to heal one crippled man reveal about God's dealings with all sinners?

4. Read John 5:14. What warning did Jesus give the healed man when he found him in the temple? How might Luke 11:24–26 relate to Jesus's warning?

5. Read John 5:16. What was wrong with the Jewish leaders that they ignored the healing of a cripple and instead criticized a Sabbath day healing? What similar things have happened in the Christian church?

6. What does the cripple's immediate trouble with the authorities indicate about what new believers can expect in this life?

7. What things in your life would make you hesitate if asked, "Do you want to be healed?"

7

Angel: Why Are You Looking among the Dead for One Who Is Alive?

1. If the women knew they were not strong enough to roll away the stone, why did they bother to go to the tomb?

2. Explain why the angel was (or was not) unduly harsh with the women.

3. What does it mean that Jesus arose from the dead in light of God's curse: "You were made from the soil, and you will become soil again" (Genesis 3:19)?

4. Read Mark 12:24. What are the two basic reasons that people deny the possibility of Jesus's resurrection?

5. Why should it help convince us of their truthfulness that Matthew, Mark, Luke, and John each give a somewhat different account of Jesus's resurrection?

6. Read 1 Corinthians 15:12–19; Acts 17:18, 31, and 25:18–19. What sort of Christian is one who does not believe that Jesus is now alive?

7. "What is your only hope in life and in death?" (*Heidelberg Catechism*, question 1)